RAISE AWARENESS with Crafts

by Ruthie Van Oosbree

raintree
a Capstone company — publishers for children

Raintree is an imprint of Capstone Global Library Limited, a company incorporated in England and Wales having its registered office at 264 Banbury Road, Oxford, OX2 7DY – Registered company number: 6695582

www.raintree.co.uk
myorders@raintree.co.uk

Text © Capstone Global Library Limited 2025
The moral rights of the proprietor have been asserted.

All rights reserved. No part of this publication may be reproduced in any form or by any means (including photocopying or storing it in any medium by electronic means and whether or not transiently or incidentally to some other use of this publication) without the written permission of the copyright owner, except in accordance with the provisions of the Copyright, Designs and Patents Act 1988 or under the terms of a licence issued by the Copyright Licensing Agency, 5th Floor, Shackleton House, 4 Battle Bridge Lane, London, SE1 2HX (www.cla.co.uk). Applications for the copyright owner's written permission should be addressed to the publisher.

Edited by Jessica Rusick
Designed by Sarah DeYoung and Denise Hamernik
Media Research by Rebekah Hubstenberger
Projects by Ruthie Van Oosbree, Aruna Rangarajan, and Chelsey Luciow
Originated by Capstone Global Library Ltd

ISBN 978 1 3982 5563 0

British Library Cataloguing in Publication Data
A full catalogue record for this book is available from the British Library.

Acknowledgements
We would like to thank the following for permission to reproduce photographs:
Adobe Stock: Prostock-studio, 4; Mighty Media, Inc.: project photos. Design Elements: iStockphoto: Bakai, Dmytro Synelnychenko, mightyisland; Mighty Media, Inc.

Every effort has been made to contact copyright holders of material reproduced in this book. Any omissions will be rectified in subsequent printings if notice is given to the publisher.

All the internet addresses (URLs) given in this book were valid at the time of going to press. However, due to the dynamic nature of the internet, some addresses may have changed, or sites may have changed or ceased to exist since publication. While the author and publisher regret any inconvenience this may cause readers, no responsibility for any such changes can be accepted by either the author or the publisher.

Contents

Crafting for awareness 4
Sign of support 6
Postcard activism 8
Brilliant badges 10
Awareness accessory 12
Cookie campaign 14
Mini mindfulness jars 16
Stitch a slogan 18
Donation station 20
Zingy zine 24
Bee aware garden 28
    Find out more 32
    About the author 32

Crafting for awareness

Do you want to change the world? Start by raising awareness! Whether you're hoping to raise funds for an organization, discuss important issues or simply get the word out about a cause, the crafts in this book will help you advocate for change. Plus, these projects are great fun to make and share. You'll love raising awareness in your community!

What is craftivism?

Craftivism is the act of using crafts to make a change in your community. It is short for "craft activism". People make crafts to protest against issues, draw attention to causes and help build a better world. Craftivism can be used for social justice, environmentalism, peace and more. Use the projects in this book to become a craftivist for any cause you're passionate about!

BASIC SUPPLIES

cardboard * coloured paper *
glue * felt-tip pens *
old magazines *
packing tape * paint *
pencil * ruler *
scissors * string

Craftivism tips

1. Prepare. Collect all your materials and supplies and read through the instructions carefully before starting a project. Cover your workspace with newspaper or another covering to protect it from spills.

2. Ask first. Before you start crafting, get permission to use any supplies you find.

3. Stay safe. Ask an adult for help using hot or sharp tools or hammers. Place scrap wood under items before hammering holes into them to protect surfaces.

4. Clean up. Tidy up after you've finished crafting. Put supplies back where you found them and clean up your workspace.

5. Keep it temporary. Craftivism projects shouldn't permanently alter public spaces. Respect these spaces and be considerate towards other people!

Sign of support

Show support for a cause, organization or value that's important to you with a bold banner!

Supplies
- cardboard
- craft knife
- clear packing tape
- paint and paintbrush (optional)
- coloured paper
- duct tape
- scissors
- black permanent marker pen
- steel wire or 2 wire hangers
- wire cutters

1. Cut a cardboard rectangle about 75 cm long and 50 cm wide for the sign. Or tape smaller pieces of cardboard together with packing tape.

2. Paint the sign a solid colour and leave it to dry. Or cover the sign in a large piece of coloured paper.

3. Use pieces of duct tape to make patterns on the sign. If you like, paint a word across the duct tape.

4. Draw letters of a word or slogan on coloured paper. Cut the letters out and glue them onto the sign.

5. Use the marker pen to add accents around the words, such as outlines and cross-hatch patterns.

6. If you like, repeat steps 2 to 5 on the opposite side of the sign to make it double-sided.

7. Cut and straighten two 60-cm lengths of wire. Carefully insert the wires into the bottom of the sign. Push them at least 15 cm into the cardboard.

8. Cover the edges of the sign in packing tape. Cut slits in the tape near the wires and wrap the tape around the wires.

9. Cover the rest of the sign with packing tape to make it waterproof.

10. Place the sign in your front garden to support your cause!

Postcard activism

Make a change with post! Whether you hand them out at school or design them for an organization's mailing campaign, these postcards are bound to have a powerful impact.

Supplies
- thin cardboard boxes, such as cereal boxes or snack boxes
- ruler
- scissors
- old magazines
- paint
- glue stick
- felt-tip pens (optional)
- pen

1. Cut postcards 15 cm long by 10 cm wide out of the cardboard boxes.

2. Cut out letters, words, patterns and images from the magazines that fit the theme of the postcards.

3. Plan out each postcard by arranging the magazine cutouts on them. Paint the printed side of the postcards and let them dry.

4. Glue the magazine cut-outs in place on the painted side of the postcards. If you like, write words on your postcards using felt-tip pens.

5. If you'll be sending the postcards by post, use the pen and ruler to draw a vertical line on the plain side of the postcard. This will separate the message and address.

6. Write a message on the left side of the line. To send a postcard, write an address on the right side of the line. Leave room for a stamp in the top-right corner!

CRAFTIVISM TIP

Many organizations have postcard-mailing campaigns. These organizations typically provide addresses for you to send your postcards to!

Brilliant badges

With DIY button badges, you can wear your support for any cause on your sleeve – or on your backpack, your jacket or a tote bag!

Supplies

- button badges
- self-adhesive badge pins
- pencil
- white paper
- coloured and decorative paper
- glue stick
- scissors
- coloured pencils
- felt-tip pens
- hot glue gun (optional)

1. Separate the back from the front of a button badge. With a pencil, trace the smaller circle several times on white paper.

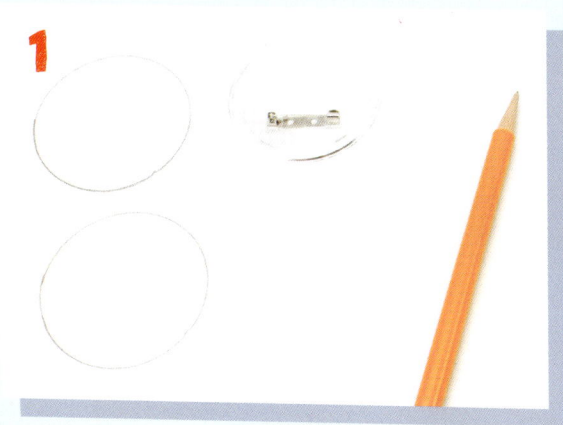

2. Cut circles or other shapes out of coloured and decorative paper. Glue the paper shapes to the white circles to design the buttons.

3. Finish the designs by adding words or drawings with coloured pencils and felt-tip pens.

4. Cut the designs out and trim the edges to fit snugly into the front section of a badge.

5. Place the designs into the front section of the badge. Push the back and the front together. Use the hot glue gun to glue the pieces together if needed.

CRAFTIVISM TIP

Make multiples of two or three designs. Then sell or hand out the badges at a fundraiser for the cause!

Awareness accessory

Many different illnesses, disabilities and causes have coloured ribbons to represent them and help build awareness. Use clay to design your own awareness ribbon bracelet for any cause!

Supplies

- polymer clay
- craft knife
- small metal jump ring
- elastic string
- ruler
- scissors
- beads

1. Choose a cause that has an awareness ribbon. You can search different ones online. Preheat the oven to the temperature indicated on the clay package.

2. Make a pea-sized ball of clay in the colour associated with your chosen cause. Roll the ball into a tube. Flatten the tube. Then trim the edges with the craft knife.

3. Poke the jump ring through the flattened clay piece. Gently fold the clay into an awareness ribbon shape. Bake the ribbon and ring according to the directions on the clay package. Let the ribbon cool.

4. Cut a 25-cm piece of elastic string. Fold the string in half. Put the folded end through the jump ring to make a loop.

5. Pull the loose ends of the string through the loop. Pull tight to make a knot.

6. String both elastic strands through one bead. Then string beads onto each separate strand.

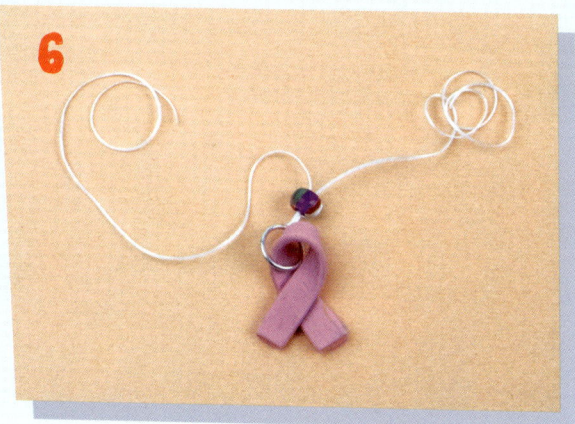

7. Once the bracelet is long enough to wrap around a wrist, knot the two ends together. Wear your bracelet to show support and raise awareness!

Cookie campaign

Decorate cute biscuits into shapes related to any cause that's important to you, such as wildlife conservation. Then sell the biscuits at a fundraiser that helps the cause.

Ingredients

- 500 g plain flour (plus more for rolling)
- ½ teaspoon baking powder
- ¼ teaspoon salt
- 175 g caster sugar
- 175 g softened butter
- 1 large egg
- 2 teaspoons vanilla extract

Supplies

- measuring spoons and scales
- mixing bowls
- mixing spoons
- greaseproof paper
- rolling pin
- cookie cutters
- baking trays
- icing (white and black)
- gel food colouring
- storage container

1. Mix the dry ingredients in one mixing bowl and the wet ingredients in another. Pour the wet ingredients into the dry ingredients and stir until smooth.

2. Place the dough onto lightly floured greaseproof paper. Roll the dough 0.5 cm thick with a lightly floured rolling pin. Chill the dough for two hours.

3. Once the dough has been chilled, preheat the oven to 180°C.

4. Cut the dough into shapes. Arrange the shapes onto a clean baking tray, leaving space between each one.

5. Bake the cookies for 11 to 12 minutes or until lightly browned. Allow the biscuits to cool completely before decorating.

6. Add white icing to small mixing bowls and colour them with gel food colouring. Decorate the biscuits. Use black icing to add details such as eyes or noses.

7. When the icing dries, carefully stack biscuits in a storage box or cake tin with greaseproof paper between the layers. Sell the biscuits at a cake sale or fundraiser!

Mini mindfulness jars

Shaking a glitter jar and watching the glitter settle can help people to relax and feel less anxious. Raise awareness about mental health and help people improve their wellbeing with these fun and calming mini glitter jars.

Supplies

- small, plain glass jars with lids
- paint and paintbrushes
- clear PVA glue
- glitter in assorted colours and sizes
- mixing spoons
- water
- food colouring
- spoon
- hot glue gun
- scissors
- coloured card
- hole punch
- pen
- string

1. Paint the lids in solid colours and let them dry. Then paint fun designs on the lids.

2. Fill one jar about one-quarter full with the glue. Add two spoonfuls of glitter.

3. Fill the jar with water, leaving a small amount of space at the top. Add two drops of food colouring to the mixture and stir to combine.

4. Use the hot glue gun to glue around the lip of the jar. Screw the lid on.

5. Repeat steps 2 to 4 with the remaining jars.

6. Cut small rectangles out of coloured card and punch a hole on one side of each. Write a mindful message on each rectangle. Use coloured string or ribbon to tie a message to each jar.

7. Give the mini mindfulness jars to friends and family so they can have a mindful moment whenever they need it!

Keep crafting!

You could add different types of glitter or materials, such as sequins, to your jars. Also, try adding more or less glue. Does the glitter settle at a different rate?

Stitch a slogan

Raise awareness in style! Spread the word about a cause that's important to you by stitching a slogan or symbol onto a piece of clothing or an accessory.

Supplies

- item to embroider, such as a T-shirt, hat or tote bag
- white coloured pencil or chalk
- fabric paint
- pencil
- black fabric marker pen
- embroidery thread in two colours
- scissors
- ruler
- needle

1. Use the white coloured pencil or chalk to outline your design on the item. Fill in the outline with fabric paint and let it dry.

2. Use the pencil to draw the outline of a word in your design. Go over the word outline with black fabric marker pen and colour in the letters.

3. Cut a 60-cm length of embroidery thread. Tie a knot in one end and thread the needle with the other end.

4. Make one stitch along the outline of the first letter. Bring the needle up a stitch-length away from this stitch. Then push the needle back down at the end of the first stitch. This is called a backstitch. Continue backstitching to outline all of the letters. Then tie a knot on the back of the item and cut off extra embroidery thread.

5. If you like, you can use other colours of embroidery thread to stitch other designs onto the item.

6. Wear your embroidered item to raise awareness for your cause!

Donation station

Supplies
- 3 rectangular boxes of different sizes
- tape
- 3 large sheets of white paper or butcher paper
- craft knife
- pencil
- scissors
- ruler
- felt-tip pens
- glue stick
- paper fastener
- decorative paper
- decorative tape
- stickers
- foam letters or letter stickers
- duct tape

Raise money for new library books or a favourite organization with a creative and colourful tiered donation box.

1. Tape each box closed. Use the large sheets of paper to wrap the two smaller boxes like gifts.

2. Use the craft knife to cut the top and sides on one end of the large box. The end should now be a flap. The flap will allow you to retrieve the donations collected.

3. Stack the boxes in size order with the largest on the bottom. Decide how you'd like the boxes to line up. Then draw a narrow slot on the top of the top box for inserting money or donation slips. Draw larger slots on the top of the bottom two boxes and the bottom of the top two boxes.

4. Wrap the bottom box with the large paper. Cut and fold the paper around the flap separately.

5. Cut a strip of paper about 10 cm long. Glue one end of the strip to the bottom of the flap.

6. Make a fold about 12 mm from the other end of the strip. The folded portion is the tab. Hold the tab on the top of the bottom box. With the craft knife, cut a slit through the tab and the top of the box. Insert the paper fastener into the slit to hold the flap closed.

Project continues on the next page.

7. Use the craft knife to cut out the slots you marked in step 3.

8. Trace the top and sides of any box you would like to cover onto decorative paper. Cut the pieces out and glue them onto the boxes.

9. Make tears in the decorative paper covering the holes in the boxes. Fold the paper into each hole and tape it down inside.

10. Decorate the boxes using felt-tip pens, stickers, decorative tape and more.

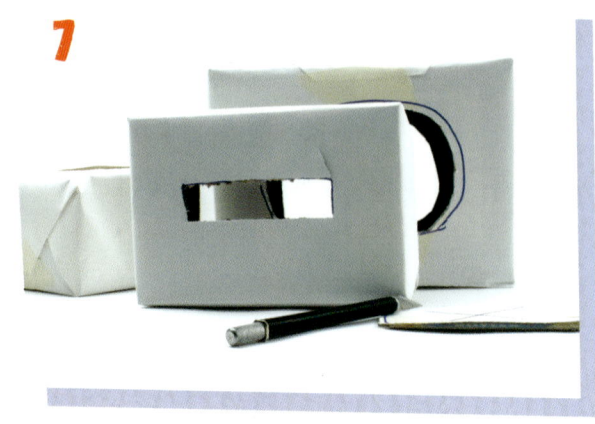

Keep crafting!

Customise your donation box for different causes! Make two boxes – one for cats and one for dogs – and ask people to "vote" for their favourite animal, giving their donations to an animal shelter.

11. Attach foam letters or letter stickers to large white labels to spell out a name or phrase related to your cause. Attach the labels to the boxes.

12. Roll duct tape into loops and attach them to the bottoms of the top two boxes. Stack the boxes so the holes align and the duct tape holds the boxes in place. Your tiered donation box is ready to raise awareness!

CRAFTIVISM TIP

Always ask for permission to display a donation box at a fundraiser or other event. Monitor the donation box to ensure the donations stay safe. When the event is over, ask a trusted adult to help you deliver the donations to the organization you raised money for.

Zingy zine

Zines are handmade, self-published magazines shared with small audiences. They can include stories, poems, recipes, comics and more. Write a zine on a topic that's important to you!

Supplies
- scratch paper
- pencil
- coloured paper
- white paper
- old magazines
- scissors
- glue stick
- paint pens
- marker pen
- felt-tip pen or ballpoint pen
- coloured pencils (optional)
- photocopier (optional)
- sewing needle
- string

1. Make a rough draft of your zine. Stack two to three sheets of scratch paper horizontally and fold them in half from side to side. Use a pencil to plan the zine's layout on these pages, adding more scratch paper if necessary.

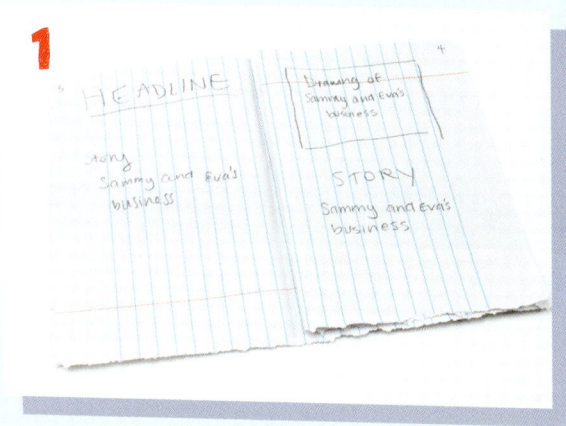

2. Stack sheets of white paper horizontally on a sheet of coloured paper. Use as many white papers as you did scratch papers. Fold the stack in half from side to side.

3. Cut out letters from old magazines to spell out the zine's title. Glue the title to the cover. Decorate around the title with magazine cut-outs, coloured paper, paint pen accents and more.

4. Write "Written and illustrated by" at the bottom of the cover in marker pen. Underneath, write your name in paint pen. Cut out a square of white paper to fill the centre of the cover. Glue it in place. Decorate any remaining blank space with stickers, magazine cut-outs and other decorations.

Keep crafting!

Add more writing space to your zine by gluing white paper to the inside of the cover.

Project continues on the next page.

5. Use felt-tip pens to draw an illustration on the white square on the cover.

6. Write a draft of your zine text in a notebook or on scratch paper.

7. For a story layout, use magazine cut-outs and felt-tip pens to add a title to the top of a page. Then write a sentence describing the story under the title in felt-tip pen or ballpoint pen.

8. Sketch out an illustration for the story on scratch paper. It should be small enough to fit in the layout you planned.

9. Draw the illustration in felt-tip pen or coloured pencil on white paper and cut it out. Glue it onto a piece of coloured paper and cut around it.

10. Glue the illustration into the zine. Then use the felt-tip pen or ballpoint pen to neatly transfer the story draft to the zine.

11. Keep adding sections to the zine until it is finished.

12. If you like, use a photocopier to make double-sided copies of each page of your zine. You can also scan the zine and print out the scanned files. Or make multiple copies of the zine by hand.

13. If using a photocopier, stack the zine pages together in order and fold them in half from side to side.

14. Thread the needle with string and pull it so both lengths of string are even. Tie the ends together in a knot. Sew down the centre of one zine. Finish on the back with a knot and cut off extra string.

15. Repeat step 14 with the other zine copies. Hand them out to family, friends and anyone else who is passionate about your zine topic!

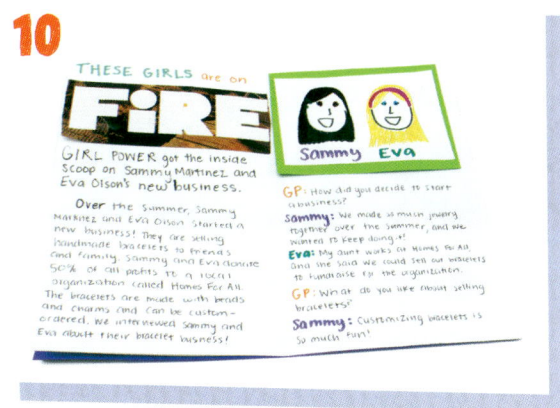

CRAFTIVISM TIP

Host a gathering to release your zine! Or get permission to share it at an event related to the zine's topic.

Bee aware garden

Pollinators such as bees and butterflies are essential to our environment. Plant a garden to help them survive while spreading the word about the importance of pollinators!

Supplies
- large bucket
- hammer and nail
- spray paint
- acrylic paint and paintbrushes
- clear coat exterior spray paint
- decorative paper
- ruler
- scissors
- glue stick
- white card
- felt-tip pens
- 2 skewers
- packing tape
- plastic recyclables
- soil
- pollinator plants

1. Ask an adult to help you make holes in the bottom of the bucket with the hammer and nail. The holes will allow water to drain out of the bucket.

2. Spray paint the bucket in a solid colour of your choice that is not light green or yellow. Let it dry.

3. Paint light green stems and leaves along the bottom of the bucket with acrylic paint.

4. Paint yellow circles above each stem for the centre of flowers.

5. Use several colours to paint petals onto each flower. Paint bees and butterflies above the flowers.

6. Spray clear coat exterior spray paint over the bucket and let it dry.

Project continues on the next page.

7. Make a sign for the garden. Cut two rectangles of decorative paper about 15 × 18 cm. Glue them together back-to-back.

8. Cut two rectangles of white coloured card about 10 × 13 cm. Write "Pollinators Welcome!" or a similar message on each rectangle with felt-tip pens.

9. Glue one coloured card rectangle to each side of the decorative paper.

10. Use packing tape to attach the skewers to one side of the sign. Fully cover the sign in packing tape to make it waterproof.

11. Place the recyclables at the bottom of the bucket to help prevent the soil from becoming too compact.

12. Fill the bucket with potting soil, leaving about 15 cm of space at the top.

13. Remove the pollinator plants from their cartons and gently pull at the root balls to loosen them. Place the plants on top of the soil. Add soil to cover the root balls of the plants.

14. Water the plants, being careful not to overwater them. Then push the pollinator sign into the soil. Place the bucket outside where people – and pollinators – can see your garden!

CRAFTIVISM TIP

Make multiple pollinator gardens and share them with other people! Offer one to a friend or neighbour. Or ask a local community centre if they will accept one as a donation.

Find out more

Books

Can You Save an Endangered Species? (You Choose: Eco Expeditions), Eric Braun (Raintree, 2021)

Create With Cardboard (Eco Crafts), Marcy Morin and Heidi E. Thompson (Raintree, 2022)

Mini Projects to Style Your Space (Mini Makers), Megan Borgert-Spaniol (Raintree, 2024)

Websites

www.bbc.co.uk/cbbc/curations/bp-arts-and-crafts-collection
Love crafting? Head for the CBBC Blue Peter arts and crafts collection.

www.booktrust.org.uk/news-and-features/features/2019/november/here-are-the-young-activists-that-can-make-the-world-a-better-place/
Read about some young activists to get inspired.

About the author

Ruthie Van Oosbree is a writer and editor who loves making crafts. She is passionate about social justice, animal welfare and the environment. She lives with her husband and three adorable cats.